D1555890

By the same author

Modern Rail Album

BR Diesels and Electrics Around Britain

TRAINS OF THOUGHT

Edited for the
Phoenix Railway-Photographic Circle
by A. W. HOBSON

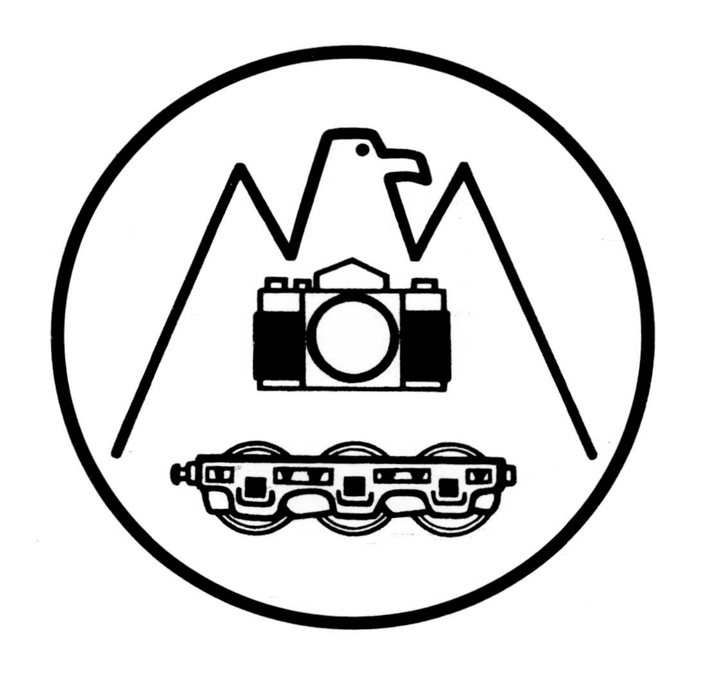

London
GEORGE ALLEN & UNWIN
Boston Sydney

First published 1981

GEORGE ALLEN & UNWIN LTD
40 Museum Street, London WC1A 1LU

British Library Cataloguing in Publication Data

Trains of thought.
1. Railroads – Great Britain – History – 20th century – Pictorial works
I. Hobson, A. W. II. Phoenix Railway Photographic Circle
385′.0941 HE3018 80–41881

ISBN 0–04–385081–2

Set in Goudy by Bedford Typesetters Ltd
and printed in Great Britain
by The Alden Press, Oxford

A Cravens class 105 d.m.u. enters Millbrook as the 13.10 Bletchley–Bedford on 10 November 1979. (*Geoff Dowling*)

INTRODUCTION

This latest collection of work by members of the Phoenix Railway-Photographic Circle takes a stage further the Circle's exploration of new pictorial approaches to railway-photography in the era of diesel and electric traction, an exploration begun in PRPC's portfolios at its foundation in 1971, and continued in its published volumes. As ever, the accent is on seeing the train in relation to its environment; no attempt is made here to cover all the locomotive or multiple-unit classes of British Rail, London Transport, or the railways of Ireland, or to give equal coverage to the various parts of these systems. Rather the photographs have been chosen for their depiction of trains in the context of place, situation, weather conditions, or the people using or observing the railway at work; and some of the section-titles reflect this emphasis. We hope that the reader will derive many hours of pleasure from leafing the pages of this book: whether as a result of suddenly seeing an aspect of the total railway environment in a new way, or whether by, as it were, glimpsing the familiar as if for the first time.

A. W. HOBSON

WATERSIDES

A Derby-built class 108 d.m.u. forming a Barrow service rumbles across Arnside viaduct on a sunny evening in September 1976. (*David A. Flitcroft*)

(*Above*) A familiar location from a slightly less familiar viewpoint. Class 52 no. 1018 'Western Buccaneer' heads along the sea wall at Teignmouth with the 08.55 Newquay–Newcastle on 14 June 1969. (*Stanley Creer*)

(*Below*) A class 25 climbs past Old Colwyn on the up line, in stormy weather on 9 August 1979. (*Larry Goddard*)

(*Left*) A Swindon-built class 120 cross-country d.m.u., on a working from Shrewsbury, passes Northgate Lock, Chester, on 23 May 1978. (*Larry Goddard*)

(*Below*) The 10.27 Looe–Liskeard branch train, formed of a Swindon class 120 d.m.u. and a Pressed Steel class 121 single unit, approaches Sandplace on 18 August 1977. (*T. G. Flinders*)

(*Above, left*) Class 47/0 no. 47.158 skirts the Birmingham–Worcester Canal near Birmingham University, at the head of the 10.35 Leeds–Paignton on 2 June 1977. (*Geoff Dowling*)

(*Left*) In freezing conditions on Christmas Eve 1979, the 13.10 Longbridge–Four Oaks cross-city service, formed of a Derby class 116 d.m.u., leaves University station, Birmingham. (*P. J. Shoesmith*)

(*Right*) A class 50 (before the naming of the class) heads a West of England express near Savernake. (*John Vaughan*)

(*Above, left*) Threading the long strip of land between the Kennet & Avon Canal and the River Avon, a Metro-Cammell class 101 d.m.u., forming the 12.15 Weymouth–Bristol, runs down towards Bath on a bright afternoon in March 1977. (*G. F. Gillham*)

(*Below, left*) Class 205 Hampshire 3-car d.m.u. no. 1103, forming the 14.56 Portsmouth Harbour–Bristol Temple Meads, leaves Redbridge on 17 April 1974, passing the point where the waters of the River Test empty into the head of Southampton Water. (*P. J. Fowler*)

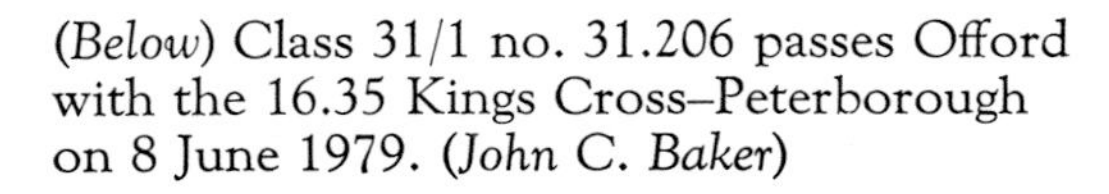

(*Below*) Class 31/1 no. 31.206 passes Offord with the 16.35 Kings Cross–Peterborough on 8 June 1979. (*John C. Baker*)

ARCHES

(*Above*) Two class 47s on china clay trains, seen from the goods shed at Lostwithiel.
(*John Vaughan*)

(*Right*) Class 45/0 no. 45.042 heads the Sunday 13.45 St Pancras–Derby semi-fast through the sequence of bridges near Kentish Town on 13 March 1977.
(*Les Nixon*)

(*Above*) Class 50 no. 50.040 tops the 1 in 101 climb to Houghton, between Preston and Blackburn, with the 10.05 Birmingham–Glasgow, diverted to run via the Settle and Carlisle route on Sunday 16 March 1975. (*David A. Flitcroft*)

(*Left*) Class 45/0 no. 45.046 heads the empty stock of a St Pancras–Sheffield express towards Nunnery Sidings, Sheffield, on 17 April 1979. (*Les Nixon*)

(*Above*) A class 40 heads a fully-fitted Edinburgh Millerhill–Carlisle Kingmoor freight over Shankend viaduct, on the northern approach to Whitrope summit on the now closed Waverley route, in May 1966. (*P. W. Robinson*)

(*Below*) A diverted Glasgow–Euston express coasts downhill from Ais Gill summit and across Arten Gill viaduct, double-headed by a pair of class 50 diesels, on 12 September 1971. (*Stanley Creer*)

(*Left*) A class 37 heads a southbound freight over the River Wear at Sunderland Bridge, Durham. (*E. C. Salthouse*)

(*Right*) Class 40 no. D221 'Ivernia', still in its original BR green livery, heads a southbound freight over Galgate viaduct, south of Lancaster on the West Coast Main Line, on 21 August 1972. (*A. W. Hobson*)

(*Left*) A class 47, taking the West London line with an Oxford–Brighton excursion train, crosses the Thames at Battersea in June 1978. (*Stanley Creer*)

When the Chester & Holyhead Railway built the North Wales Coast main line in the 1840s, the thirteenth-century town walls at Conway were breached by means of a handsome archway, through which class 47/4 no. 47.555 'The Commonwealth Spirit' is seen heading the 10.05 Holyhead–Euston on 1 June 1979. (*Larry Goddard*)

(*Above*) A Swindon class 124 trans-Pennine d.m.u., forming the 18.55 Liverpool Lime Street–Hull, climbs high over the River Tame and the Ashton Canal as it crosses Saddleworth viaduct on 31 July 1977. (*Larry Goddard*)

(*Left*) During the celebrations of the bicentenary of the Ironbridge Gorge, in 1979, a special Sunday service was provided to Coalbrookdale, on a now normally freight-only branch, for visiting tourists. Here a class 116 d.m.u., bearing the West Midlands PTE logo, sets out from Coalbrookdale with a return working for Wolverhampton, on 26 August. (*P. J. Shoesmith*)

MIST

In the winter gloom of 16 December 1976, a Deltic crosses Durham viaduct with the 08.00 Edinburgh–Kings Cross express. (*R. Elsdon*)

Awaiting a clear road for the run to depot for servicing after arrival from the north, a class 45 stands in St Pancras station early on the morning of 25 January 1977. (*Paul Clark*)

(*Above*) Class 47 no. 1818 stands in the yard of the closed station at Caernarvon on New Year's Day, 1971, during the period in which the Menai Bridge–Caernarvon branch was reopened to serve a temporary Freightliner depot, following the disastrous fire on the Britannia Bridge in May 1970.
(*A. W. Hobson*)

(*Right*) At 1.50 am on the freezing night of 4–5 December 1976, the 'Western China Clay' railtour, headed by no. 1023 'Western Fusilier', pauses at platform 1 at Swindon station. The weather conditions have deterred travellers on the special from the usual rush to the head of the train to take photographs, and through the mist the guard is approaching to enquire whether the one lone worshipper wishes to board the train!
(*T. G. Flinders*)

(*Above*) A class 47 heads a westbound van train into watery afternoon sunlight near Little Bedwyn in October 1975. (*Philip D. Hawkins*)

(*Right*) On a foggy day in December 1975, class 25/2 no. 25.175 makes its way past Wandsworth Common, returning from Norwood Junction with an inter-regional freight for Willesden. (*Stanley Creer*)

(*Right*) A class 52 heads the 08.35 Penzance–Paddington past Langport on 26 February 1973. (*P. J. Fowler*)

(*Below*) Sunlight is gradually piercing the mist as a class 205 Hampshire d.m.u., forming a Bristol–Portsmouth service, passes Sydney Gardens, Bath, on 10 December 1976. (*P. J. Fowler*)

SNOW

(*Left*) With a thin covering of snow capping the Pennine foothills in the background, class 45/0 no. 45.052 heads a Manchester–Leeds football excursion past Greenfield Junction, near Stalybridge, on 25 February 1977. (*Les Nixon*)

(*Below*) With the embankments stilled by snowfall, a Victoria–Maidstone East train, formed of two class 414/3 2-car e.m.u.'s and a class 411/2 unit, runs towards Bickley on 29 December 1976. (*Brian Morrison*)

(*Above*) Class 25/2 no. 25.169 heads a freight past Totley Tunnel East signal-box and towards Totley tunnel, on 24 February 1979. (*T. G. Flinders*)

(*Left*) A diesel multiple-unit of mixed stock, forming the 11.05 Bedwyn–Reading, pulls away from Hungerford on 28 December 1976. (*T. G. Flinders*)

(*Left*) Class 47/3 no. 47.311 approaches Hexham on 17 February 1979 with a train of ICI Anhydrous Ammonia tanks for Carlisle. (*Brian Morrison*)

(*Above*) Class 31/2 no. 31.293 passes Thurston, as it runs back light to Ipswich after working a train of empty vans, for sugar-beet pulp workings, to Bury St Edmunds on 24 January 1979. (*John C. Baker*)

(*Above*) A late-afternoon train, formed of a class 108 d.m.u., rolls into Hawarden, on the Bidston–Wrexham branch, in the bright but bitter cold of 20 March 1979. (*Larry Goddard*)

(*Above*) Class 24 no. D5134 shunts at Bangor on 3 January 1970. (*A. W. Hobson*)

(*Below*) A Metro-Cammell class 101 d.m.u., forming the 12.20 Manchester Victoria–Hull, at Diggle on New Year's Day, 1980. (*Les Nixon*)

GLIMPSES

(*Left*) Through a car window, as a fellow-enthusiast pauses for a carton of fish and chips and a class 45 heads an express past the former Sawley Junction, now renamed Long Eaton. (*John East*)

(*Below*) Through the latticework of a railway footbridge at Highworth Junction, near Swindon: class 47/0 no. 1726 at the head of the 15.25 Cardiff–Paddington on 16 April 1976. (*T. G. Flinders*)

(*Right*) Through a window of the derelict goods shed at Lostwithiel: a class 47 on a china clay working edges past. (*John Vaughan*)

(*Below*) Through the gloomy overbridges of Birmingham New Street: 20.160 works through with a brake-van on 2 November 1979. (*Geoff Dowling*)

(*Above*) Through a broken window on the footbridge at Clapham Junction: 33.114 on pilot duties in February 1977. (*John Glover*)

(*Right*) From a footbridge at Bolton station: a BRC&W Class 104 d.m.u. approaches on a Manchester Victoria–Southport service, on 30 August 1979. (*David A. Flitcroft*)

(*Below, right*) Through the bars of a BRUTE truck on a platform at Birmingham New Street: class 47/0 no. 47.201, after arrival with a train from the south-west on 10 April 1976. (*David A. Flitcroft*)

(*Right*) Over a fence near the ARC Conbloc Works siding, Nuneaton: the driver of 08.536 takes a rest from shunting, with temperatures in the mid-70s, on 19 May 1977. This siding was formerly part of the Ashby & Nuneaton Joint line from Abbey Junction to Burton-on-Trent. (*Kevin Lane*)

47 20

UNDER THE WIRES

(*Above*) The 04.25 from St Pancras arrives at Manchester Piccadilly behind class 46 no. 150 on 10 April 1968. (*R. Elsdon*)

(*Right*) Class 31/0 no. 31.008 trundles a freight for Temple Mills yard through Stratford on 26 May 1977. (*Kevin Lane*)

(*Above*) A class 31 lifts the empty stock of an incoming Anglo-Scottish sleeper train past Caledonian Road, on the line out of King's Cross, as electrification work is completed, on 29 May 1977. (*J. A. Howie*)

(*Left*) A class 47 heads a train of Ford Motor Company parts past Stratford on 29 March 1978. (*Michael H. C. Baker*)

(*Left*) A class 304 e.m.u., and catenary supports, at Lichfield on 17 March 1972. (*P. J. Shoesmith*)

(*Centre*) The 12.40 Fenchurch Street–Shoeburyness, formed of class 302 e.m.u. no. 283, runs into Upminster on 26 May 1977. (*Kevin Lane*)

(*Bottom*) A telephoto view of up and down morning peak-hour services on the Moorgate–Welwyn Garden City route, on 8 June 1977. The trains are formed of class 313 e.m.u.'s. (*Michael H. C. Baker*)

(*Left*) Class 76 no. 76.051 emerges from the western end of Woodhead tunnel with a train of coke hoppers on 1 September 1977. (*Geoff Dowling*)

(*Below*) Loaded hoppers of coal awaiting shipment stand under the catenary at St Hilda's Sidings, on the NCB's Westoe Colliery Electric Railway, South Shields, in March 1975. (*E. C. Salthouse*)

INDUSTRIAL

(*Above*) A class 45 speeds past Manvers coking plant and the entrance to Manvers Main Colliery, on the Leeds–Sheffield route, with an up express on 27 July 1979.
(*Les Nixon*)

(*Left*) A class 101 d.m.u. on High Level bridge, Newcastle, with a South Shields–Newcastle local service on 27 August 1978. In the middle distance can be seen the King Edward bridge, and the new Tyneside Metro viaduct under construction.
(*Geoff Dowling*)

(*Right*) A class 101 d.m.u., forming a Darlington–Saltburn service, heads away from Middlesbrough in April 1977.
(*P. W. Robinson*)

An unidentified class 45 approaches Trent Junction with an express in 1976, passing the array of immense cooling-towers at Ratcliffe-on-Soar power-station. (*Les Nixon*)

(*Right*) A meeting of old and modern at Rufford Colliery sidings, a spur off the former Midland Railway Mansfield–Newark line: class 20 nos 20.136 and 20.134 head a loaded coal train from Clipstone sidings towards Mansfield, past the old Midland Railway cabin and signals, on 14 April 1977. (*Les Nixon*)

(*Above*) Outside the Gretton Brook shed of BSC's Corby Ironstone Quarries railway system, 0–6–0 diesel-hydraulic no. 62, formerly BR class 14 no. D9515, is refuelled before retiring 'on shed' after the day's operations, on 7 October 1976. (*Kevin Lane*)

(*Right*) Yellow-liveried 204-hp 0–6–0 diesel-mechanical no. 4 of the Tees & Hartlepools Port Authority, formerly BR class 03 no. D2024, shunts on the dockside at Middlesbrough in April 1977. (*P. W. Robinson*)

(*Above*) A service on the Bolton–Manchester Victoria route, formed of class 104 and class 101 d.m.u.'s, passes Cohen's Scrapyard, Salford, on 12 June 1979. The Cohen's yard shunter, an 0–4–0 diesel-mechanical (John Fowler no. 23009 of 1944) stands alongside the line. (*Kevin Lane*)

(*Below*) No. 850, a four-wheeled diesel-hydraulic (Thomas Hill no. 166V of 1966), operated by Tube Investments Ltd at Chesterfield, shunts between the works and the BR exchange sidings on 7 June 1979. (*Kevin Lane*)

URBAN

(*Above*) The 11.41 from Stratford Low Level, formed of a 3-car d.m.u. of mixed stock, arrives at North Woolwich in May 1976. The skyline of London Docks can be seen in the distance, and in the foreground is the desolate ground once occupied by the railway goods yard. (*Michael H. C. Baker*)

(*Left*) A class 101 d.m.u., forming a service out of Glasgow Queen Street, climbs Cowlairs bank on 31 August 1979. (*Les Nixon*)

(*Right*) The Thames and Westminster are glimpsed between buildings on the South Bank, as class 405/2 4-SUB e.m.u. no. 4651, on a Richmond–Waterloo working, passes Vauxhall on 16 February 1976. (*Michael H. C. Baker*)

(*Above*) Another hybrid d.m.u. on the North Woolwich branch is seen leaving Stratford Low Level, on 26 May 1977. (*Kevin Lane*)

(*Below*) Elsewhere in the Inner London suburbs, a class 116 d.m.u. on a Kentish Town–Barking service is glimpsed near Upper Holloway on the gloomy morning of 9 June 1977. (*Kevin Lane*)

The summer of 1976, though one of the driest on record, was nonetheless not without its damper moments: in a torrential rainstorm on 28 August, class 47/4 no. 47.435 emerges from under the north bridge at Doncaster with the 10.30 Edinburgh–Kings Cross. (*David A. Flitcroft*)

(*Above*) A class 105 d.m.u., forming a Blackburn–Manchester Victoria service, approaches Bolton just as a class 108 unit makes a smoky exit from the carriage sidings to form the 16.22 for Kirkby, on 1 June 1977. (*David A. Flitcroft*)

(*Above, right*) A class 25 heads a freight on to the ex-LNWR Timperley–Garston line at Arpley Junction, Warrington, passing a class 24 on shunting duties, on 27 December 1975. (*Mike Esau*)

(*Right*) A view from Shrewsbury Castle of a class 47 approaching on the Wellington line with a freight, on 28 August 1975. (*Michael H. C. Baker*)

(*Left*) With the Birmingham city skyline silhouetted against early evening sky, a class 86 heads the 18.48 Euston express past Adderley Park station on 15 August 1978. (*P. J. Shoesmith*)

ARPLEY JUNCTION
Royal Mail
TAXI
4088

(*Above*) A class 47 heads the 15.55 Swansea–Paddington past Briton Ferry on 10 March 1973. (A. W. *Hobson*)

(*Above, left*) A refurbished class 108 d.m.u., forming a Leeds–Huddersfield working, descends towards Batley on 25 May 1977. (*Les Nixon*)

(*Below, left*) Class 40 no. 318 passes Shotton with the 15.28 Bangor–Euston on 19 July 1973. (A. W. *Hobson*)

(*Right*) A class 120 cross-country d.m.u., forming the 12.16 for Swansea, leaves Newport on 20 February 1977; in this view it is about to enter Hillfield tunnel. (*Les Nixon*)

(*Above*) Class 40 no. 40.053 heads the 11.35 Glasgow–Aberdeen over the Tay viaduct out of Perth on 14 May 1977. (*Chris Dyke*)

(*Opposite, above*) A Derby class 115 d.m.u. heads a St Pancras–Bedford stopping service out of St Albans on 19 December 1979; some catenary support-masts for the forthcoming electrification are already in position. (*Kevin Lane*)

(*Opposite, below*) Class 31/1 no. 31.188 heads past a faded graveyard in Leicester with a brake-van on 20 December 1975. (*R. Elsdon*)

(*Right*) Glimpsed from a pathway down the side of The Mound, a class 08 diesel shunter performs pilot duties at the east end of Edinburgh Waverley station on 20 April 1975. (*R. Elsdon*)

The morning express from Glasgow and Edinburgh to Manchester passes Moses Gate, near journey's end, behind class 47/4 no. 47.555 on 1 June 1977. (*David A. Flitcroft*)

(*Above*) Class 25/1 no. 25.050 crosses Stoneclough Road, Kearsley, with a haul of empty coal wagons from Kearsley power-station on 18 November 1974. (*David A. Flitcroft*)

(*Below*) Class 52 no. D1047 'Western Lord' leaves Taunton with a westbound special on 21 March 1970. (*R. Elsdon*)

OUTSKIRTS

(*Above*) In the last years of the class 52 diesel-hydraulics, one of their regular workings was the 13.12 (conditional) freight from Norwood to Acton, which ran two or three times a week. Here no. 1058 'Western Nobleman' heads the train past Tooting Bec Common, near Balham Junction, South London, on 12 September 1976. (*Stanley Creer*)

(*Left*) Class 50 no. 50.031 heads a southbound freight from the Manchester area along the West Coast Main Line near Winwick Junction, Warrington, on 2 August 1974. GEC Traction's Vulcan works, and part of the village, can be seen in the distance. (*David A. Flitcroft*)

(*Right*) Also at Tooting Bec Common, class 47/0 no. 47.072 is glimpsed at the head of an inter-regional excursion for Brighton on 30 April 1977. (*Stanley Creer*)

(*Right*) Class 415/1 4-EPB e.m.u. no. 5223, forming the 12.32 Dartford–Cannon Street, leaves Mottingham on 15 January 1976. (*Brian Morrison*)

(*Above, left*) Light-running class 25/1 no. 25.042 runs past Crane Street, on the outskirts of Chester, on 19 June 1979. (*Larry Goddard*)

(*Below, left*) Class 47/4 no. 47.418 approaches Scout tunnel, Mossley, with a York–Liverpool express on 23 June 1979. (*Les Nixon*)

(*Below*) Class 40 no. 40.176 trundles an eastbound mixed freight along the Irwell Valley between Farnworth and Kearsley on 13 November 1979. (*David A. Flitcroft*)

Deltic no. 55.011 'The Royal Northumberland Fusiliers' heads the 14.05 Kings Cross–York near Grantham on 14 July 1979. (*Les Nixon*)

Near Lostock Junction, Preston, class 25/2 no. 25.112 rolls a brake-van towards Wigan, and the late afternoon sun, on 20 September 1974. (*David A. Flitcroft*)

An unidentified class 45 passes Ratcliffe-on-Soar power-station (just out of picture on the left) with a down express on 7 May 1977. (*Les Nixon*)

COUNTRYSIDE

(*Above*) In a typical East Anglian landscape, a 2-car d.m.u. forming the 18.48 from Norwich is seen near Yarmouth on 11 July 1979. (*Geoff Dowling*)

(*Right*) A breeze caresses the railway embankments near Mossley as the 14.47 York–Liverpool sweeps by behind 47.544 on 22 September 1979. (*David A. Flitcroft*)

(*Above*) A class 101 4-car d.m.u., forming a Haltwhistle–Alston train, approaches Lambley station on 23 April 1976, one week before the branch's closure. (*Les Nixon*)

(*Above, left*) An unidentified class 47 heads an Edinburgh–Kings Cross express away from Chaloners Whin Junction, near York, on 12 June 1976. (*Les Nixon*)

(*Left*) One of the last regular class 52 passenger duties was the 08.25 (Summer SO) Paddington–Fishguard. Only two months before withdrawal, no. 1009 'Western Invader' heads the train near Shrivenham, Wiltshire, on 24 July 1976. (*T. G. Flinders*)

(*Right*) A class 101 2-car unit, forming the 15.35 Leeds–Morecambe, near Bell Busk on the climb to Hellifield on 25 July 1979. (*Les Nixon*)

(*Above*) Caught by a brief sunny period on an otherwise overcast day, the 09.15 Penzance–Plymouth, formed of a Pressed Steel class 121 single unit railcar and 3-car d.m.u., crosses Tregeagle viaduct, near Truro, on 13 September 1979. (*G. F. Gillham*)

(*Right*) A class 108 d.m.u., forming the 12.30 Manchester Victoria–Blackburn, crosses Wayoh viaduct, north of Bolton, on 5 August 1974. (*David A. Flitcroft*)

(*Above*) A class 108 d.m.u., forming the 16.57 Llandudno–Holyhead stopping train, near Malltraeth, Anglesey, on 20 July 1973. (*A. W. Hobson*)

(*Above, left*) A class 37 locomotive, with a brake tender, shunting the exchange sidings at Whittle Colliery, Northumberland, in the winter of 1974. (*E. C. Salthouse*)

(*Left*) Class 45/0 no. 45.022 ‘Lytham St Annes’ roars down the rain-sodden fells with the 10.45 Glasgow–Nottingham via the Settle and Carlisle route, on 13 September 1976. The train has just crossed Arten Gill viaduct and is about to enter the northern portal of Blea Moor tunnel. (*T. G. Flinders*)

(*Right*) An unidentified class 47 heads north through rural Durham with an express for Newcastle, during the winter of 1976. (*E. C. Salthouse*)

STATIONS

(*Left*) An engineer's train of soiled ballast, headed by class 40 no. 40.003, rumbles through the former Manchester Exchange station, now largely disused other than as a car park, on 1 September 1975. (*David A. Flitcroft*)

(*Opposite*) On a cold but sunny morning in January 1976, a class 108 d.m.u., forming the 11.37 Rochdale–Manchester Victoria via Oldham, passes over the junction with the Stalybridge line at Miles Platting station, and approaches the steep bank into the city. (*David A. Flitcroft*)

(*Right*) At platform 11 at Manchester Victoria (the platform formerly continuous with Manchester Exchange) a train for North Wales, formed of Park Royal class 103 and BRC&W class 104 d.m.u.'s, prepares to leave on 28 April 1979. (*Les Nixon*)

15

(*Left*) Class 45/0 no. 45.049 'The Staffordshire Regiment (The Prince of Wales's Own)' prepares to leave Exeter St David's with the 07.50 Derby–Truro on 16 April 1976. (*Cyril Lofthus*)

(*Right*) Class 52 no. 1065 'Western Consort' awaits a clear road for the run light to Old Oak Common, after arrival at Paddington with an express on 3 October 1975. (*Cyril Lofthus*)

(*Below*) Front ends: a line-up of class 502 e.m.u.'s and class 105 and 108 d.m.u.'s at Liverpool Exchange station in April 1977. (*Mike Esau*)

1A93

(*Left*) Sunday morning calm at Lincoln Central on 24 October 1976, with a class 108 d.m.u. and a class 47 at rest. (*P. J. Shoesmith*)

(*Opposite, above*) Through the increasingly lush undergrowth surrounding the disused goods station at St Pancras, class 45/1 no. 45.128 is seen leaving the main-line station with an afternoon express made up of newly allocated air-conditioned stock, in September 1976. (*John Glover*)

(*Opposite, below*) A class 105 d.m.u. loads a healthy complement of returning shoppers at Blackburn station before leaving for Colne, in June 1974. (*Stanley Creer*)

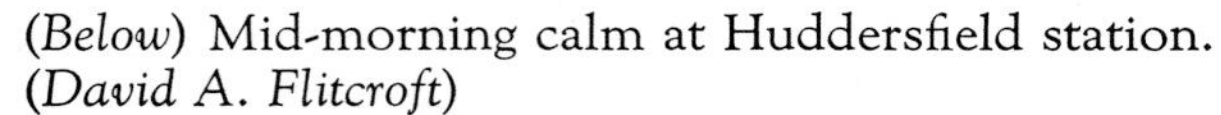

(*Below*) Mid-morning calm at Huddersfield station. (*David A. Flitcroft*)

Way out
2 →

(*Left*) Sunshine, litter and a class 86, at Crewe station. (*John East*)

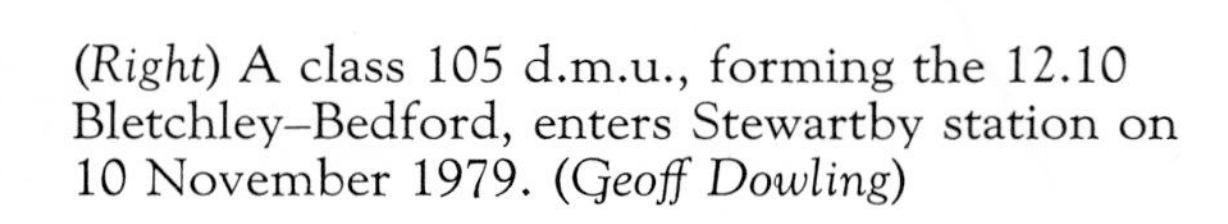

(*Right*) A class 105 d.m.u., forming the 12.10 Bletchley–Bedford, enters Stewartby station on 10 November 1979. (*Geoff Dowling*)

Class 25/1 no. 25.050 pauses at Gleneagles with the 13.38 Dundee–Glasgow Queen Street, on 28 May 1977. (*Brian Morrison*)

(*Left*) Deltic no. 55.010 'The King's Own Scottish Borderer' heads the up 'Flying Scotsman' through a very wet York station on 5 January 1977. (*David A. Flitcroft*)

(*Opposite*) Two views of Alston station on a cold wet day in October 1975, with a class 101 d.m.u. forming the shuttle service for Haltwhistle. (*John Glover*)

(*Below*) Two class 491 4-TC non-powered units, forming part of the 13.46 Waterloo–Bournemouth, as it pauses at Winchester during a sunlit rainstorm in January 1976. (*John Glover*)

13

ALSTON

(*Left*) A deserted Mirfield station on 5 September 1979, with 47.500 'Great Western' speeding by at the head of a York–Liverpool train. (*David A. Flitcroft*)

(*Below*) Class 45/0 no. 45.018 drifts through Bedminster station, on the run into Bristol Temple Meads with the 15.10 Plymouth–Leeds train on 18 September 1974. Little remains of the station beyond two overgrown islands and small, spartan, metal and glass shelters; it is used for only a few minutes each day by commuters to and from the city. (*P. J. Fowler*)

(*Left*) Nuneaton, 8 December 1979: a discarded tail-lamp, and 86.255 working the 12.05 Liverpool–Euston. (*Geoff Dowling*)

(*Below*) Chatham station in a downpour, 23 June 1978: train indicators, and class 411/2 no. 7171 leading the 11.38/11.40 Ramsgate/Dover–Victoria. (*Brian Morrison*)

(*Left*) A pair of Class 414/3 2-HAP e.m.u.'s at Brighton station on the evening of 7 June 1979, after arrival as the 19.04 from Eastbourne. (*Cyril Lofthus*)

(*Above, right*) An Inter-City arrival from Euston, headed by class 86/2 no. 86.250, and a class 116 d.m.u. forming a local service, at Birmingham New Street on 2 April 1977. (*Brian Morrison*)

(*Below, right*) Inter-City 125 unit no. 254.022, forming the 12.50 from Kings Cross, awaits departure from Leeds on the last stage of its journey to Harrogate on 5 September 1979. (*David A. Flitcroft*)

(*Below*) An unusual combination of telephoto lens and binoculars was used for this picture of a class 47 leaving Reading with an up express on 9 August 1975. (*Paul Clark*)

(*Left*) A class 103 e.m.u. at Glasgow Central station on 15 April 1974. (*R. Elsdon*)

(*Right*) Middlesbrough station on a sunny day in September 1974, with a pair of class 101 d.m.u.'s approaching on a Saltburn–Darlington working. (*D. Griffiths*)

(*Below, right*) Pale sunlight filters through the windows at Kings Cross on the morning of 27 December 1976, as Deltic no. 55.009 'Alycidon' stands at platform 3 with express stock. (*Stanley Creer*)

(*Below*) In freezing temperatures, class 31/4 no. 31.411 stands at the buffer-stops while on station pilot duties at Kings Cross on New Year's Day, 1979. (*Stanley Creer*)

(*Above*) The 13.12 Nottingham–St Pancras is restarted from the ex-Midland Railway station at Kettering by class 45/1 no. 45.110 on 12 July 1979. (*Kevin Lane*)

(*Below*) A class 50 stands at Birmingham New Street with the 18.25 for Paddington via Oxford on a sunny afternoon in April 1977. (*Mike Esau*)

(*Above*) A Derby-built d.m.u., forming a Carlisle service, at Newcastle station in July 1977. (*E. C. Salthouse*)

(*Below*) A class 405/2 4-SUB e.m.u. pauses briefly at Clapham Junction with a Waterloo service in May 1973. (*Michael H. C. Baker*)

Way out
Walting room
G
400
21

(*Right*) A class 26/1 leaves Garve station, in the Scottish Highlands, with the 17.45 Inverness–Kyle of Lochalsh, on the rainy evening of 3 June 1977. (*Les Nixon*)

(*Left*) Class 86/0 no. 86.022 arrives at the refurbished Oxenholme station, on the edge of the Lake District, with the morning Glasgow/Edinburgh–Birmingham train on 26 June 1978. (*David A. Flitcroft*)

(*Below*) A class 108 d.m.u. forming the 10.34 Pwllheli–Shrewsbury, pulls away from Harlech, on the Merionethshire coast, on 19 April 1979. (*David A. Flitcroft*)

(*Above*) A busy scene at Doncaster station on 28 August 1976. On the down fast line, class 47/4 no. 47.482 restarts a northbound extra after a crew-change; at platform 5, class 46 no. 46.011 pauses with a Kings Cross–Hull train; at platform 6 stands a class 104 d.m.u. which has just arrived with a local service from Hull; class 31/4 no. 31.417 stands silently in a siding between duties; and class 40 no. 40.168 arrives at platform 8 with a northbound parcels train. (*David A. Flitcroft*)

(*Right*) Class 52 no. 1028 'Western Hussar' leaves Banbury with the 06.45 Paddington–Birmingham on 7 August 1976, passing a class 116 d.m.u. on an up local service. (*T. G. Flinders*)

(*Left*) The evening sun catches a class 101 d.m.u. as it leaves Machynlleth for Aberystwyth on 25 July 1972. (*G. F. Gillham*)

(*Right*) A class 47 runs light through Arnside station, on the Furness line, en route for workshops for attention on 10 June 1974. The trackbed on the left is of the abandoned branch to Hincaster Junction, on the West Coast Main Line. (*Stanley Creer*)

(*Below, right*) Another view of Arnside station, this time on 27 June 1978: a class 108 d.m.u. approaches, forming the 13.51 Barrow–Preston. (*David A. Flitcroft*)

(*Below*) Class 423 4-VEP e.m.u. no. 7733, forming a Bournemouth–Waterloo stopping service, leaves Sway station, in the New Forest, in August 1976. (*John Glover*)

6P39

A Pressed Steel class 117 suburban d.m.u., forming the 13.45 Treherbert–Llandaff service, leaves Dinas Rhondda on 20 February 1977. (*Les Nixon*)

Stranraer Harbour station on 2 June 1977, with class 25/2 no. 25.084 standing at the head of an up parcels train, and a line of new Hillman Avenger cars waiting to be loaded for the sea-crossing to Larne. (*Brian Morrison*)

A class 117 d.m.u., forming a service for Coryton, pauses at the near-derelict terminus at Cardiff Bute Road on 22 August 1979. (*Les Nixon*)

A class 105 d.m.u. stands at the largely demolished station at Bedford St Johns, before departure for Bletchley on 21 July 1979. (*Stanley Creer*)

TRAVELLERS

PLATFORM Nº
PLATFORM Nº 10
WOKING
BASINGSTOKE
ANDOVER
GRATELEY
SALISBURY
Change at Basingstoke for the above stations
To ensure the punctual departure of trains this barrier will be closed immediately before the train is due to leave
Inter-City
7
3114

(*Above*) Class 419 electric motor luggage van no. 68003 in Dover Priory station sidings on 22 April 1976. (*A. W. Hobson*)

(*Above, right*) A passenger waits for a Midland line express service at Leicester station, as a class 104 d.m.u., forming the 11.16 for Peterborough, is loaded on 4 June 1977. (*Michael H. C. Baker*)

(*Right*) Stock on display outside Derby Works on Open Day, 1977 – including a withdrawn class 17 and one of the first production batch of Metro-Cammell d.m.u.'s – is glimpsed from a train approaching Derby station from London. (*J. A. Howie*)

(*Opposite*) Passengers queue at Waterloo to board a Portsmouth train, formed of 4-COR e.m.u. no. 3114, in August 1970. (*Mike Esau*)

(*Above*) The relief driver walks past waiting passengers as the 17.00 Waterloo–Exeter, headed by class 33/1 no. 33.109, rolls to a halt at Salisbury on 29 July 1976. (*G. F. Gillham*)

(*Right, above*) A class 101 d.m.u. leaves Darlington for Stockton on a bright morning in October 1975; platform-ticket holders, having seen off family or friends, make for the barrier. (*Mike Esau*)

(*Right*) A scene at Sheffield Midland in January 1975. (*P. W. Robinson*)

3

6a
Waiting room

A waiting off-peak passenger on a sunny but cold day at Barnes. (*Mike Esau*)

(*Above*) A lone passenger makes her way to the class 104 d.m.u. forming the 14.45 for Derby, at Nottingham Midland on 20 September 1969. (*R. Elsdon*)

(*Below*) Class 414/3 2-HAP e.m.u. nos 6112 and 6132, forming the 13.28 Margate–Charing Cross via Deal, approach Sandling on 12 June 1976. (*A. W. Hobson*)

(*Left*) Intending passengers anticipate the arrival of the 10.37 Rochdale–Manchester Victoria train at Failsworth on 29 January 1976, as the 10.50 Manchester–Rochdale climbs into the station. Both trains are formed of class 105 d.m.u.'s. (*David A. Flitcroft*)

(*Right*) Watford West station is served by the peak-hour-only Croxley Green e.m.u. service. Here the shuttle train, formed of a class 501 unit, departs as the alighting passengers make their way out of the station, on 20 April 1977. (*John Glover*)

(*Below, right*) A rest on a convenient trolley in the sun at Carlisle station on 3 June 1977, as station pilot 08.911 shunts. (*Brian Morrison*)

(*Below*) With the platforms crowded with holidaymakers, the 08.32 Halifax–Hull, headed by a class 104 d.m.u., arrives at Scarborough on 11 August 1979. (*David A. Flitcroft*)

B9
WARNING

08 911

(*Left*) Class 121 single-unit railcar no. W55034, forming the 18.16 Bristol Temple Meads–Severn Beach, about to continue from Montpelier station to Redland, the next call on the branch, on a sunny evening in May 1974. (*P. J. Fowler*)

(*Above, right*) Two elderly passengers wait for a Swanage train at Corfe Castle during the last months of the branch's operation. The d.m.u. is a class 205 Hampshire 3-car unit. (*Mike Esau*)

(*Below, right*) A class 108 d.m.u. forming the 13.50 Leeds–Huddersfield rumbles into Dewsbury station on 5 September 1979. (*David A. Flitcroft*)

CORFE CASTLE
1105

Way out
Waiting room

WATCHERS

Class 25/1 no. 25.042 about to leave Manchester Victoria with a d.m.u.-replacement service for Oldham. (*Geoff Dowling*)

(*Above*) HST unit no. 253.013, forming the 09.00 Bristol–Paddington, draws the attention of two youngsters as it enters Swindon on 24 October 1976. (*T. G. Flinders*)

(*Below*) To the alarm of at least one young traveller, HST unit no. 253.007 roars through Swindon as the 09.00 Swansea–Paddington on 19 February 1977. (*T. G. Flinders*)

SPOTTERS

(*Above*) Kings Cross in October 1975, with enthusiasts looking on as Deltic no. 55.011 'The Royal Northumberland Fusiliers' departs with the 18.00 for Newcastle. (*Michael H. C. Baker*)

(*Above, left*) Spotters discuss spottings while a class 47 and a class 52 look on; Paddington, 11 April 1974. (*Kevin Lane*)

(*Left*) Spotters, and a class 103 d.m.u., warm themselves a little in the winter sun on the afternoon of 29 January 1977. (*D. Griffiths*)

(*Right*) Young enthusiasts pick their way over the shells of the cabs of class 44 no. D3 'Skiddaw', at Derby Works Open Day, 1977. (*J. A. Howie*)

(*Left*) Spotters strain to see the number of class 85 no. 85.036, as it stands in a loco siding at Birmingham New Street on 2 April 1977. (*Brian Morrison*)

(*Right*) The dusk is gathering, but a few of the hardier spotters still linger as 85.039 sets off southward from Nuneaton with a ballast train on 29 October 1976. (*P. J. Shoesmith*)

(*Below, right*) The platform at Paddington is chock-a-block with jostling enthusiasts as class 52 no. 1023 'Western Fusilier' prepares to leave with the 'Western Memorial' railtour to Chester and Crewe on 29 January 1977. (*Michael H. C. Baker*)

(*Below*) Class 304 and 310 e.m.u.'s, and a solitary enthusiast, at the southern end of Birmingham New Street on 10 May 1975. (*D. Griffiths*)

85 039
85 039

RAILWAYMEN

(*Above*) A look-out man, and a class 40, in Holloway sidings, London, in May 1970. (*Michael H. C. Baker*)

(*Above, left*) A class 105 d.m.u. on a Bedford St Johns–Bletchley working rattles off into the distance as the Lidlington crossing keeper opens the gates to traffic once again; 14 April 1976. (*Kevin Lane*)

(*Left*) After the early arrival of the 13.00 Kings Cross–Edinburgh at Doncaster on 7 August 1976, the guard pauses for a chat with a permanent way man. (*T. G. Flinders*)

(*Right*) A Kings Cross porter, September 1971. (*Michael H. C. Baker*)

SIDINGS

Red Bank sidings, Manchester, on 10 November 1979. (*Les Nixon*)

(*Above*) Old Oak Common carriage-sidings; in the foreground, more spotters await a 'Western' railtour. 26 February 1977. (*Michael H. C. Baker*)

(*Below*) Coton Hill sidings, Shrewsbury, and the main line northwards to Chester, seen from Shrewsbury Castle on a sunny morning in August 1975. (*Michael H. C. Baker*)

(*Above*) Kings Cross fuelling depot on 7 March 1977. The three Deltics include nos 55.020 'Nimbus' and 55.012 'Crepello'. (*Les Nixon*)

DEPOTS

(*Right*) A class 37 stands by at the head of the Cambridge Engineer's train, near the motive power depot on the night of 20 July 1969. (*R. Elsdon*)

(*Above, right*) Leicester motive power depot on 4 June 1977, with a characteristic array of class 45s and class 25s, and LMS signals on the adjacent main line. (*Michael H. C. Baker*)

(*Right*) Two class 56s and two class 20s outside Toton m.p.d. on Open Day, 9 June 1979. (*Les Nixon*)

(*Left*) Two class 52s at Exeter stabling point on 21 July 1975. (*D. Griffiths*)

OLEO
OLEO
OLEO

BLOCK TRAIN MISCELLANY

(*Above*) A class 17 enters Alloa with a coal train off the Dunfermline line, in October 1966. (*P. W. Robinson*)

(*Above, left*) Class 47/3 no. 47.380 passes Shirebrook Colliery with a northbound empty merry-go-round working on 28 August 1979. (*Les Nixon*)

(*Left*) Another class 47 approaches Ferrybridge power-station with a loaded merry-go-round working on 19 November 1979. (*Les Nixon*)

(*Right*) Class 45/0 no. 45.063 passes Abbey Junction, Nuneaton, with oil tankers for Birmingham on 19 May 1977. (*Kevin Lane*)

(*Above*) A pair of class 25s head the eastbound Tilcon company train (07.30 Rylstone–Hull) through Castleford on a May morning in 1974. (*John Glover*)

(*Below*) A northbound block oil-train, headed by 47.047, slows to cross over to the fast line at Harpenden Junction on 24 November 1977. (*Kevin Lane*)

(*Above*) A class 40 climbs past Slattocks, between Manchester and Rochdale, with an Ellesmere Port–Leeds Neville Hill oil-train, in July 1976. (*David A. Flitcroft*)

(*Below*) Class 25/2 nos 25.160 and 25.161 approach Cheddleton tunnel, near Leek, with a northbound mineral working from Oakamoor on 1 June 1979. (*Les Nixon*)

OVERGROUND

Units of London Transport's 1967 Victoria Line stock are used on the Central Line's Woodford–Hainault shuttle-service, in turn with the Central's 1960 stock. A single 1967 set pauses at Roding Valley on 1 November 1979. (*Kevin Lane*)

(*Above*) A train of 1938 stock leaves Neasden for Stanmore on 9 June 1977. (*Kevin Lane*)

(*Below*) Blake Hall station, on the LT Epping–Ongar branch, is situated in the most rural of surroundings. In this view, a train of 1962 stock leaves with a mid-morning working to Epping in March 1977. (*John Glover*)

IRISH SCENES

(*Above*) A General Motors class 141 Bo-Bo heads away from Killiney with the 13.55 Dundalk–Bray stopping train on a bright afternoon in March 1977. (*R. Elsdon*)

(*Above, left*) Crossing the River Barrow at Monasterevan with the 13.30 Dublin Heuston–Cork, on 12 July 1974, are General Motors Bo-Bo diesels nos B172 and B188. (*R. Elsdon*)

(*Left*) General Motors Bo-Bo no. 205 arrives at Dublin Lansdown Road with the 08.52 Bray–Balbriggan stopping train on 22 March 1977. (*R. Elsdon*)

(*Right*) An AEC/Park Royal d.m.u., headed by car no. 2620 and forming the 13.50 Bray–Dublin Connolly, between Killiney and Dalkey on 31 May 1971. (*R. Elsdon*)

(*Left*) On arrival at Howth station, passengers with their children leave for an afternoon by the sea, while the locomotive secondman takes the tail-lamp to the rear of the train, a push-pull set operated by Bo-Bo no. 211, in preparation for the return journey to Bray. 23 June 1977. (*Kevin Lane*)

(*Right*) Howth Junction on Christmas Eve 1979, with the 11.10 Dublin Pearse–Balbriggan push-pull train entering the station. (*Michael H. C. Baker*)

(*Below, right*) Dublin's Connolly station, the same day, with the 11.00 'Enterprise' express for Belfast, formed of a BREL d.e.m.u., departing. (*Michael H. C. Baker*)

(*Below*) General Motors no. B203 arrives at Dublin Connolly with the 10.28 Bray–Howth on 6 May 1977. (*R. Elsdon*)

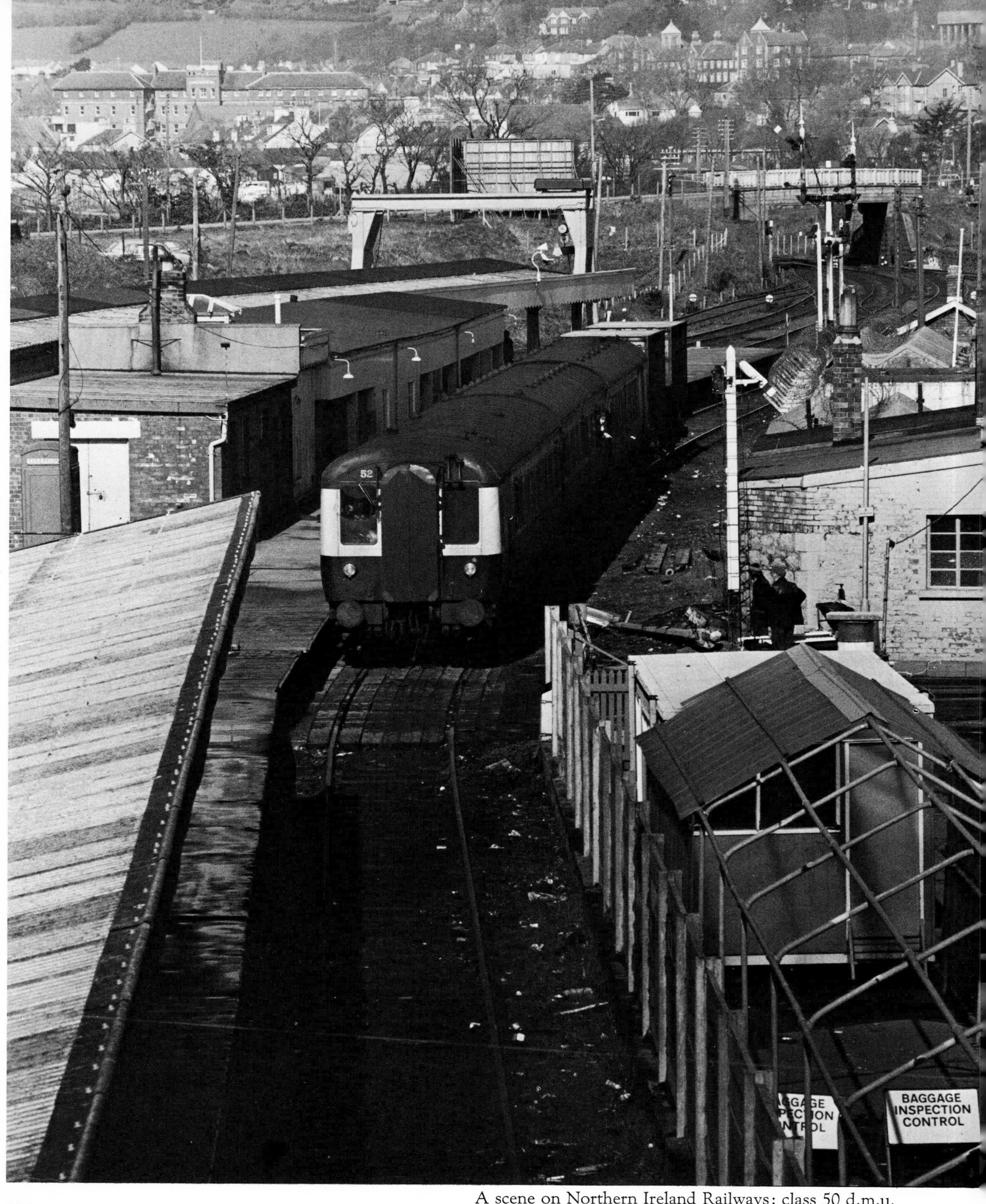

A scene on Northern Ireland Railways: class 50 d.m.u. no. 52 arrives at Larne station with a boat-train working at Easter 1977. (*E. C. Salthouse*)

(*Above*) Two General Motors class B Bo-Bos wait to back down onto a freight for Ballinacourty, at Waterford North in August 1976. (*Michael H. C. Baker*)

(*Below*) A line of General Motors class B Bo-Bos, together with a class A and a diesel shunter, outside Inchicore m.p.d., Dublin, on 30 September 1972. (*R. Elsdon*)

SUNSET

(*Left*) A class 52 heads the St Blazey–Stoke freight up the southern slope of Dainton bank on 14 September 1975. (*Stanley Creer*)

(*Below*) A view of Corfe Castle from a d.m.u. approaching from Wareham, during the last years of the Swanage branch. (*Mike Esau*)

A Redhill–Reading d.m.u. heads into the setting sun between Gomshall and Shalford on a February afternoon in 1974. (*Mike Esau*)

SCRAPYARD

Class 52s, and remnants of class 24s, in Swindon Works scrapyard in the late 1970s. *Valete*. (*John Vaughan*)